Anyone can do 'Easy'

An Entrepreneur's journey

by

I0461939

Dave Brazer

PUBLISHED BY:
(Davebrazer.com)

COPYRIGHT
All rights reserved. No part of this book may be reproduced or
transmitted in any form
or by any means, electronic or mechanical, including
photocopying, recording or by any
information storage and retrieval system, without written
permission from the author,
except for the inclusion of brief quotations in a review.

About the author

David is a Social Entrepreneur (Male Entrepreneur of the year 2016) with over 20 years' experience of working in, managing, founding and Directing Social projects and Social Businesses.

David established his first Social Enterprise, Citadel Associates (SY) Ltd, in 2008 which is in existence to support the most marginalised people in society into employment, training and career support.

In 2014, he established another Social Enterprise (Ignition Training Centre) (Social Enterprise of the year 2017) delivering mechanic skills along with employability support and he now runs them both. David is also a Keynote and motivational speaker and supports other entrepreneurs who want to come through and start up in business.

Unlimited Potential is Dave's Self-Development and Entrepreneurship roadshow, currently touring the North of the UK. Public Speakers College supports the development of public speaking and communication skills, from beginner to professional. We are in the information age and the art of public speaking has never been so important as it is today. From gaining a job through interview to giving a keynote speech or the presentation of your life.

David has had a varied career before becoming a Social Entrepreneur. David would say he failed his way to the top, but all served as a learning experience for his eventual success as an Entrepreneur. The following awards have been proudly won by David and his organisations over the past few years. Hopefully some of the thoughts, ideas and words in this book will help you along your journey into entrepreneurship.

Duke of York Community Initiative Award
Northern Lights Social Enterprise of the year
Male Entrepreneur of the year
Enterprising Learning Provider of the year
IDOX Innovation award
Doncaster Free Press pride award
Most innovative Project of the year
Learning Provider of the year
Vodafone World of Difference Award
BMBC Learner Champion Ambassador Award

Sarah Trouten, CEO, at the IOEE:
"From humble beginnings, David and his team have grown Ignition Training into something quite extraordinary. The work this ambitious social enterprise does has had an amazingly positive impact on so many lives, while simultaneously saving stretched local services significant amounts of money. I'd like to offer my warm congratulations to David, his team, and everyone they've helped back onto the road to independence."

Edward John Chapman – Duke of York Community Initiative:
On behalf of Ron and myself many congratulations on being successful in your application for the Award. We were both very impressed with the quite unique Ignition project, your commitment and your inspirational and participative management. I look forward to meeting you again at the Awards ceremony.

Contents

Dedication

This book is dedicated to so many people, firstly the two most important people in my life. My wonderful daughter Lois for whom I wish to be a positive role model and show her that with self-belief, hard-work and commitment, anything is possible. She was born to be better than me and she is already forging her own path. My goal is to be a major inspiration in her life. I hope she'll be as proud of me as I am of her.

And to my partner Jan, without who's love, help, support and encouragement this journey would not have been possible or indeed worth the effort. She has been my inspiration, my soul mate and all that I believe in. She said four words to me some time ago that made all the difference to my entrepreneurial journey, "I believe in you", the four words that I believe are missing in education today. Maybe children's attainment, confidence and self-belief would increase on hearing them.

Also, the dedicated and motivational people who I have considered part of my team over the years. You have inspired, challenged, supported and sometimes downright frustrated me. You've made me laugh and battled alongside me but whatever our relationship, you have each taught me something along the way and I wouldn't have missed your friendship, support, challenges or dedication for the world.

Finally, thank you to the various people in my life who have tried to put me off, tell me I can't, knock me down and ensure I failed. You made me stronger, more resilient, more determined than I could have ever been without your input. Every knock hardens me, every defeat is a lesson, every put down lifts me higher. Without all the obstacles you put in front of me I would have ended up less of a man.

Dave

Introduction

The venue was a plush hotel in Sheffield. (Yes, Sheffield does have plush hotels, that's Rotherham you're thinking of, joke). It was a dark damp and rainy November night, the type of rain that doesn't look much but soaks you through to the bone. There was an air of excitement buzzing through the carpark as the guests made their way to the hotel entrance as they caught site of the lights inside and began to hear the music.

South Yorkshire Business Awards. It was what in Yorkshire we'd call a 'posh do'. You should have seen me as I walked in the prestigious ceremony, feeling a right berk in my 'James Bond' dinner suit and pretend elastic bow tie (with a real one in my pocket for later so I could wear it loose and look cool).

I looked around nervously to check that everyone else was wearing a monkey suit, just in case I'd been the victim of a practical joke and everyone else was in fancy dress. Imagine the embarrassment if everyone was dressed as super heroes, Vickers and Tarts and I turned up in a suit. I'd have been a laughing stock. I'd been told that I was nominated for an award, but I didn't know for what category.

I'd been an Entrepreneur for 10 years and attended many of these occasions, winning a few myself. Although it was always a shock when I did. These events are always filled with inspirational people from all walks of life. That's one reason I enjoy them. There is great diversity of people and ideas to be inspired by.

We were entertained by speeches from some of the business world's 'movers and shakers', followed by a singer and a brilliant magician who amazed us with some 'impossible' illusions.

Anyway, the event had a great atmosphere, mainly due to the people. It wasn't about egos or 'psychobabble' you sometimes get at these events, just a great get together. About 200 guests were sitting at tables of 10. It had taken years to get to this point in my life. I was there with Jan on the 'odds and ends' table where we all seemed to be in couples. It was a great evening with some incredible people on our table including an ex-pilot in his 80's who couldn't stop himself chatting up every woman in sight (luckily he couldn't see that far) and many self-made entrepreneurs with inspiring stories to tell.

As with many of these events, any one of those inspirational people could have won and nobody could have said they didn't deserve it. As far as I'm concerned, if you've gone through all the heartache of building a business then you deserve the recognition for it.

As the host shouted the names of each nominee, cheers bellowed out from the nominated tables around the room with ten or more people round them. Big corporations with even bigger budgets. They finally got to my name and – complete bloody silence.

Talk about being able to hear a pin drop, we could have heard a feather drop. Jan and I looked at each other with the kind of look that said aren't we Billy no mates. We weren't going to shout on our own. Thing was, we'd done all the hard-work for all those years, so we left the shouting to the Master of Ceremonies. Then he shouted my name, Dave Brazer, Male Entrepreneur of the year. You don't have to shout to succeed.

First a reality check

So, you've decided to become an Entrepreneur, or rather like most of us, life steered you in that direction due to a burning desire to make a difference to the world, your own life, your family or at least to a local need or personal passion. Maybe you've seen a gap in the market or invented something which has solved a problem.

Here's the thing straight from the horse's mouth. Unless you're starting out with an incredible skillset, business plan and financial backing, becoming an entrepreneur is not a walk in the park (unless you're starting a dog walking business). Nor is it a means to riches for most of us. Its seriously hard-work 'up front' with no guarantee of success and for the most part, you can forget home life. You need to build skills, and a resilience which is far beyond what you currently imagine is possible. I often say that I wish I'd opened a burger van instead. Not a real option, especially considering my culinary 'disabilities'.

I know the pain and the joy of becoming an Entrepreneur, the things you'll learn, from business planning, accounts, admin, people skills, management, marketing, negotiation, website creation, social media, public speaking and a hundred other skills to stretch, terrify and inspire you. People may tell you that your idea is silly (more about them later), you won't sleep, you'll have a million rules to adhere to that you never even knew existed and to cap it all you'll get little thanks for what you do, and you will want to give in on occasion. This journey is undoubtedly not for the feint hearted.

Have I put you off yet? I hope not, because I want you to have the passion, courage and determination to succeed. The world needs more people like you, and I salute you for taking the leap of faith in yourself and your business, project or idea. The idea usually comes from something close to your heart, it needs to be to keep you motivated. If you have already started on this journey you will still be learning, the lessons never end.

You will come to understand yourself more each day along this journey you are about to undertake, and you will be rewarded personally, professionally and hopefully financially. Although my business experience is mostly (though not entirely) creating Social Enterprises, I hope the ideas, encouragement and thoughts in it can be useful to those of you who are looking at starting any business. Indeed, even a Social Enterprise needs an element of residual income generation which is earned rather than tendered for, gifted or granted. It must be sustainable beyond short term grants. This isn't a 'how to' guide as such, merely a collection of thoughts, anecdotes and ideas which I hope will help.

Thankfully there is help there, we, ourselves run a business and motivational platform 'Unlimited Potential' (unlimited-potential.org) to support you with self-development and business strategies and the good news is that today there are more opportunities than ever before, so we hope to see you at one of our events soon to tell you more. If not, there are plenty of other's out there too.

What do you want from your journey?
Financial freedom, more family time, a sense of achievement, to quit the rat-race, adoration, pride from someone, a social cause, big house, car, yacht. The answers to the above will largely answer what type of business you ultimately go into and the plans you make to get there.

By the way, history is littered with people (especially entrepreneurs) who have done the above (eventually) but found that the big house, flash car etc still left them unfulfilled. It is nice when you get the car you always wanted but it doesn't fulfil you personally.

I know many millionaires who are way ahead of me in their Entrepreneurial journey and far richer. They've had Ferraris and Porsches, but they all say the same thing, "money doesn't buy you happiness".

So, what is wrong? The truth is none of the trappings will make you happier. Oh yeah Dave I hear you say, trust me a Porsche will make me happy. Yes, I'm not denying nice things can make the difference to your life and it's far easier when you are rich than poor, but you can be rich and miserable, just as you can be poor as a church mouse and be happy. I'm merely saying think carefully about your choices and decisions as they can have a huge impact on your life, especially if you make a success of something you don't really want to be doing or something that takes you further from your 'why' the reason you started the business in the first place.

Business owners in general are one breed and can stay behind a counter in their hardware shop for decades without getting bored. Entrepreneurs generally enjoy the rush of getting things started, making it into something that nobody thought would succeed and building it. They don't however enjoy what they see as the drudgery of managing their companies, day to day stuff is a chore and they usually have more ideas than they have time to bring to fruition. There is no right or wrong here, just differences.

Which personality type are you? Are you the type to focus on one thing and be happy to run it for 20 years or are you easily bored? Are you steady and value security (in which case you may wish to start a business to make a living and stay with it) or do you constantly want to start something new for the challenge (Entrepreneur) I had an absolute fear that I would be doing the same job for years because I'd grown up with seeing my dad and his friends all going to work, working hard and staying in the same job for ever.

Strange I thought, because I noticed that paradoxically people ended up staying in jobs for life at a time when, as my Dad said, "you could tell your boss to stick it on Friday afternoon, walk out across the street and have another job to start on Monday". Nothing wrong with having a job for life though, and I wish that our young people had the option of this level of security these days, but it wasn't for me. Well I say that, but dad got me my first job and as I found, it was infinitely harder to get out of than into. I see how people get trapped in jobs.

I once thought my dad was risk averse, especially as the owner of the business Dad had been running for years decided to sell up. Dad was an electro-plater, plating that shiny chrome you see on scissors, bath taps and the like. This involved using electrolysis, using electrodes to run a current through a chemical solution. There was a particular odour, in the place, not unpleasant but you could tell, not healthy. They had large vats of water containing various deadly chemicals, nice things such as acid, cyanide and lead, chromium, nickel and zinc.

The place was a Health & Safety man's nightmare with rotten planks (walkways) between the vats, that had been corroded with the chemicals spilling onto them as Dad lifted out the scissors on jigs. Dad's trousers came home in a similar state most of the time. They had litmus paper on hand (to check acidity) but Dad was 'old school' and used to dip his finger in, taste it and say it "needed more acid", or zinc or something, like a master chef tasting a recipe. You need a degree for this job nowadays and just press a button cos its automatic.

Anyway, as a 14-year-old lad, when everything is simple, I said, "Dad why don't you buy it". It was a perfect opportunity in my head for him to own a well-established business already trading. I was amazed he said no but I didn't appreciate till years later when I had a family that he was providing for his family, my mum, me and my two sisters Sue and Michelle. Having kids to look after meant that the value of security for him was paramount and outweighed potential risk. Well, not for him but for us, his family. Thank you, Dad.

Now I have got that off my chest I invite you to look through the rest of this book and share my journey and thoughts, which has been interesting and challenging, exhausting, inspiring and sometimes heart-breaking for me to write, especially about my dad. I hope it makes you think in places, laugh in others and most of all, I hope it gives you the courage and some strategies to take control of your destiny and chase your worth.

So where do you start?

Have you ever had a great idea for a product, service or business and did nothing about it? Then sometime later you see that idea had been taken on by someone. Didn't you kick yourself? Becoming an entrepreneur of any kind is not just about having an idea, it's about committing to take that idea forward and running with it. I assume you have an idea of what you want to do, otherwise you probably wouldn't be reading this book. Maybe you've already started the business and are curious about another 'entrepreneurs' journey.

This will sound like an old cliché but maybe the single most important piece of advice I can give you if you haven't started is '**Take the first step**', if you didn't hear that I said **TAKE THE FIRST STEP**. Or as NIKE put it, '**Just do it**'. Just a slogan maybe, but 3 of the most important words of advice you will ever hear.

Oh yeah, Dave, I hear you say, if it was that easy everyone would do it. Well no, everyone wouldn't do it. Just as not everyone gives up smoking, or exercises, or loses weight, or studies for their future, or saves for retirement from the 45 years + they earn money. Most die flat broke. I lost count of the people who've come to me for employment support who haven't worked for 10 years or more and say something like "I want to be an HGV driver". I say, "how long have you had a drivers' licence"? and they say, "oh I don't have a licence" or something along those lines. If you haven't taken the first step you will not succeed in your chosen field.

All things come to those who don't wait my friend.

I promise, once you have taken the first step *with intent* you can take the next step and the next. It's a bit like walking through fog, you can't see where you are going exactly but move a step forward and you can see a little further. If you stray from your intended path you can always change direction. One day my friend, if you haven't fallen into the river, the fog will lift and you (and everyone else) will see clearly how far you've come.

Tell me, do you believe you can be a millionaire? If you don't it's probably because you've not associated with people who have become millionaires. It probably feels so far from where you are currently that it is difficult to put your mindset in that arena. Difficult but not impossible. My advice is to access their courses, books, stories, seminars etc. Follow me on DaveBrazer.com to access some of the best and most inspiring of these people.

Do you think the lone caterpillar sitting munching on a leaf understands what it's like to be a butterfly? They might be able to dream about it, but they can't really 'know' the feeling until they change into a butterfly. You need a good dose of self-belief and (as all religious books say) faith that it will happen and one day instead of being a caterpillar looking up and wondering how those butterflies have succeeded in spreading their wings and flying so freely you'll be the butterfly looking down remembering when your life had caterpillar 'limitations' and your view on life, and consequently your results were in line with those limiting beliefs.

Have you ever seen those guys fire walking along on hot coals? What do they focus on? Do you think they would even step onto the coal if they focused on every single step, they had to take along the way? not a chance! It would be too daunting a prospect. They focus on the end where they can get off the hot coals, get their feel in a bowl of water and relax. Keeping your sights set on the overall goal and purpose is essential to keep the dream alive in your heart when the times get tough.

Take positive definite steps and plan the journey but don't lose sight of the end goal. Oh, and don't stand still long enough to get your feet burned. In business, we all reach points along the way when we say "I would never have done this had I known how hard it would be. As we overcome the barriers though, our mindset alters a little more each time and we climb the next hurdle.

It isn't 'easy'
but
Anyone can do 'Easy'

don't be just anyone.

Here's a secret Entrepreneurs know

If it means something to you then don't wait until you believe in yourself to begin. Or until you are qualified. Get started and the belief comes with the culmination of the small successes and failures (lessons) in your life. It was a tough but incredibly powerful lesson for me to learn that people who told me that I 'couldn't do it' were in fact subconsciously saying that '*they couldn't do It*'.

I can tell you this, I fell in to the trap of doubting myself early on in life. I was written off by most people in childhood and consequently had little self-belief. My teachers were about as inspiring as a Justin Bieber album, the man with the vocal range of an earthworm (apologies if you're a fan, of earthworms). Our teachers couldn't know why the children didn't achieve great grades. Truth is, we simply lived up to *their* expectations of us at the time. There have been numerous studies and experiments into the effects of 'Expectations theory'. Basically, if you have positive expectations of something or someone, they will live up to your expectations of them. That also works with negative expectations. What happens when you say to a child, why are you always so clumsy? Yes, they are always clumsy.

I wasn't born into a rich, or even a 'well off' family, just a bloody hard working one. I can't say my birth was heralded by the angels. I'm told that when I was born the Doctor smacked my *mother's* arse. I started work at 16 and felt trapped in a dead-end job for years because I wasn't being true to myself by at least trying to become self-employed, that dream was for other people (excuse). Where I came from, Borstal was where everyone went on their holidays.

All I am saying is, it's much easier to run with the excuses as it absolves people from responsibility.

I've lost count of the people who come to me and say something like "nobody will give me a chance". I say, "Come in, I'll give you a chance" but they usually make some particularly ridiculous excuse and disappear by lunchtime. **You must commit to giving yourself a chance first.**

Assuming responsibility for your own life is a pre-requisite of the entrepreneur. If you assume ultimate responsibility for your own life and situation you are more likely to do something about it if it isn't going your way.

Tip - Let me tell you something up front relating to skills. If you wait until you have all the skills that you feel are necessary to succeed *you will never get the business off the ground.* You do need skills however every entrepreneur realises at some point that, and I can't stress this enough, **'Success is never about can or can't, it's always about will or won't.**

There are millions of people who can but that doesn't translate to actions. **Most people say I wish, Entrepreneurs quit the excuses and say, "I will".**

I once heard a phrase, everything you want is on the other side of fear. This is so true! Do you remember when you learned to swim? Quite a daunting thing wasn't it the first time you were coaxed into jumping in. I remember a friend of mine was terrified, His body wanted to dive in, but his brain didn't. He was left shaking while teetering on the edge of the water until he eventually fell in with a splash, freakishly causing a bloody nose as he hit it on the side on route. He now loves swimming.

Adam Peaty MBE, the first British man to win an Olympic swimming gold since1988, was afraid of the water when he was younger. Then won 4 Golds at the Commonwealth games in 2014. You must jump in 'before' you learn how to swim

What drives you forward

The answer to this is very different for each of us. Jim Rohn, the American success coach said, "Take an idiot and motivate him and all you have is a motivated idiot". I disagree with this statement. I'd rather be, (or employ) a motivated idiot than a lazy genius. Anyone who's motivated enough can achieve so much more than the sum of their parts. **It's not a skillset, it's a mindset**. It's when you are a lazy idiot that you really have problems. What's the point in having talent in any walk of life if you don't use it? Imagine Rembrandt painting and decorating for a living. Nothing wrong with decorating if that's what you really want to do, but don't sell yourself short, or write yourself off, or write anyone else off for that matter.

The thing that drove me to become self-employed was the need to follow my own path. I started my Social Enterprises after I found my passion and I was motivated by the support my organisation could give to people who had been mostly written off. This is my end goal in these businesses.

I once employed a lady who had a learning disability and had suffered from depression for 20 years. People asked why I employed her. Well I can tell you that she was lovely, didn't get into office politics, worked hard and was lovely to clients. Yes, we had to spend a bit more time teaching her the necessary skills but once she learned, her confidence improved. She's still working as a telephone interviewer for another company to this day. Self-development is very important as is supporting other's development. The rewards are incredible.

I used to go to the pub (a lot) in my younger days and hear the same people constantly moan about their job, or their husband/wife, their house, their boss or state of their neighbourhood. Think about this though, if you are truly unhappy with any of these you can change them. It just takes a decision, determination and commitment and finally action. I didn't want to be in that same pub in 20 years' time moaning about the same issues. I wager I could walk into any pup now and hear the same thing, different people. It wasn't easy though to break free, it wasn't until I was made redundant that I decided to take the opportunity to learn new skills.

Two beliefs drive me on when the going gets tough.
I hold two beliefs in myself. One is that *I never quit.* I know that success isn't about giving in, it's about trying new, sometimes innovative ways if you aren't getting results you intend. However, that mind-set (some call it stubbornness) has served me well and driven me to carry on when all I really wanted to do was to climb into bed and hibernate. When my body and mind are so exhausted, I remember this belief.

Another believe I hold which drives me is that **I must be so close to success because I'm so close to giving in**. I don't know why but life seems to work that way. It's as if God says to you "OK do you *really* want this? so "what are you prepared to endure to get there"? It's strange but it's true that the greatest success often comes just after the biggest falls or tragedies in our life. It's during the tough times when it's easy to forget this, make sure you keep it in the forefront of you mind. Tattoo it on your forehead if you must.

Your 'beliefs' are so important, so this is something else I can't stress enough. Put it this way. If you are superstitious and you 'believe' *with all your heart* that as the old saying goes, seeing one magpie is bad luck ('one for sorrow') and you see one just as you are about to walk into a job interview or a business pitch. How well do you think you will come across?

What if you had another interview the following day and saw two magpies as you walked in? this denotes, as the saying goes 'two for joy'. How differently would you hold a negotiation or interview? how much more enthusiastic would you come across? and how much more likely would you be to get the job or the business deal on this day? Even though *nothing had changed* except that you 'believed' you were about to experience either good or bad luck. Why not adopt a different belief such as 'The harder I work, the luckier I get'?

"Whether you believe you can, or you believe you can't, you're right".

Henry Ford

The Leap of faith

What about that fateful day when you get your business started? For most of us the way in is by dipping our toes in the water and starting part time while keeping our day job. I tried this approach myself in the early days, however I found that I was maybe doing things half-heartedly because I had the relative security of my job. When I started my first Social Enterprise, I just left my job which I loved and was paid quite well for (if you ignore the hours I was putting in, and the hassle I coped with).

Did you ever see the Indiana Jones films? In one of them, Indiana Jones and the last crusade, the intrepid relic hunter is searching for the Holy Grail, the cup that Jesus and his disciples used at the last supper. Legend has it that the cup possesses miraculous powers which, if drank from would provide eternal youth.

Indi had to get to the other side of a precipice to reach the Holy Grail? He had gone through numerous life-threatening obstacles to get to this point. From his point of view, he was looking down a chasm between him and the cave where the grail is sitting. The camera pans away to show the path to the other side which is visible from another point of view. Opportunities are always there too if we look from another angle, sometimes though we just don't see them.

He remembers that one of the clues he read from his father's notes was about taking a leap of faith and he throws some dust in front of him to highlight the path. Light your path by reading other people's work or get a mentor to show you the way but whatever you do, take the leap. It's strange that we are living in a society where everything is demanded immediately but we wait until retirement to 'live' life.

There are other pages in this book which elude to the jump over the cliff approach but it's an important issue because there are some questions to ask yourself. If you don't know the answer you may come to a juddering halt. Questions like am I comfortable risking everything on this venture? or How do I handle stress, rejection, gossip, ridicule, etc? and if you get knocked down 10 times how many times do you get back up?

This reminds me of the Viking leader who ordered his men to burn their boats when they reached a new land to conquer. They gave themselves no escape, so they had to win or die. Are you this positive that your venture will work? Then go for it! I'm not saying don't get advice, but the decision is yours alone when to burn your boats.

The most successful people are the ones who say they can, even when nobody ever has!

Every Great move forward in your life begins with a leap of faith

Brian Tracy

Your business is your baby

Do you have children? Were you there at the birth?
I remember the day my life changed forever. My wife and I
were ushered into a sterile room in the maternity room. She
was about to go into labour. I was shaking like a leaf inside
but telling my wife that everything was going to be alright.

What I imagined would be the most joyous experience
imaginable, I found, turned out to be the most stressful time I'd
ever had. Our baby's heart-rate kept dropping dangerously low
and we could see this ourselves on the monitor, right there
beside my wife's bed. I'd gone into the room quite excited but
that was quickly turning to trepidation. The whole scene was
organised chaos and I wasn't getting any calmer while the
midwife kept looking at the monitor and disappearing out of
the door.

Meanwhile my wife was getting a flair-up of her sciatica. For
those of you who don't know what sciatica is, the sciatic nerve
is the longest nerve in the body and runs from the hip down the
leg to the foot. It's incredibly painful when trapped, doubly so,
I assume during childbirth. So here I was, holding the wife's
hand, getting the life squeezed out of mine, and telling her
everything was going to be alright. She was screaming in pain,
asking for an epidural, and she couldn't move her leg. Added
to this, a dizzy midwife was running in and out of the room
with increasing frequency.

When the Doctor arrived, my wife couldn't move her leg and
he sent the nurse out again for stirrups (WTF). I almost made a
quip about riding but instinctively kept my gob shut. Back she
came with these two poles like the ones you tie the washing
line onto, but shorter. She put these poles into holes positioned

at the bottom corners of the bed and then she and the Doctor grabbed a leg each and while Jo screamed in agony, promptly strapped her ankles to the tops of each post. At this point I'm thinking "thank God men don't give birth" while simultaneously carrying on telling her that everything's going to be alright. And they say men can't multi-task.

Then the Doctor said to me, "come down here" I said "what, me?" as if I was one of a crowd, and found myself complying, looking like a dead man walking. He said "here", promptly handed me a torch and said, "Your job is to shine this". For some weird reason I said "where", well I was stressed out remember. The Doctor said, pointing at my groin area. "the same place you pointed THAT, 9 months ago".

As I shone the torch into the abys, I remember thinking to myself, when we married a year ago, I never envisaged that in 12 months I'd be standing shoulder to shoulder with another dude shining a torch at my wife's snatch. He then said "go on, closer man" I said "I didn't get this close during the bloody conception" trying to lighten the mood!

It got worse, he shouted "Nurse get the ventouse" which I thought was one of the Musketeers. Porthos, Aramis, D'Artagnan, Ventouse. Turned out it was basically a cross between a vacuum cleaner and a penis pump. Luckily it was the vacuum he wanted. Which was a good job as my penis shrunk 5 inches at the sight of this kit, and I only had 4 to start with.

They started the birthing process and returned me back to my comfort zone to hold my wife's hand. Then, on our side of the room something changed. **Time stopped.**

The room darkened. We didn't move a muscle but silently looked towards the other side of the room. Over there, the

24

medical staff were in bright vivid technicolour and clear, crisp surround-sound. Time was at double speed over there. I didn't say a word, I didn't have the words to say, so we just held hands as we watched them trying to 'revive' our baby.

After a while, time started to move again and sound slowly faded back through the bubble we were trapped in, when we heard a sound we'd never heard before, but we recognised it immediately. It was our new baby's cry, the most joyous sound we'd ever heard. It was as if she was saying, mummy, everything is alright.

Moral of the story, my daughter was my first baby, my business, it turns out, was my second. All the elements are there when you conceive and give birth to a business. The anticipation, excitement, fear, pain, trepidation, heartache, bluffing to convince your nearest and dearest that everything will be alright, the emotional worry and then, the incredible, overpowering pride.

I have a picture of me looking so proud holding my daughter that day and I've been proud of her for the past 24 years. Thank you for letting me re-live this moment again with you.

What about competition?

OK so you have your business idea and your setting out as an entrepreneur. It's a wonderfully exciting time for you and a little scary too. It's easy to become bogged down in feeling that it's 'you against the world'. Someone asked me at a recent talk I did about starting a business "what about competition".

Just remember, you are not really in competition with everyone, or anyone for that matter. There are now around 7.4 *billion* people on planet Earth. I had the audience do this exercise. You can do it too.

Imagine yourself sitting in front of a cinema screen and every one of those people on Earth are represented on the screen by a dot, with you represented by a dot in the centre. Over 7 billion dots. Not much white left on the screen is there? Now take away the dots that represent everyone outside the country you live in, then subtract everyone outside your town or city, then those people who are not in your immediate vicinity, then the people outside the age range or ability for employment. All the time seeing those dots disappearing, leaving more white space on the screen as you go.

Now take away all those who are happily employed or have no interest in the business you are creating, and finally, from the ones who are left, take out the ones who are without the will, skills, finances and passion to take the business forward. Not so many people left in competition with you now are there!

Yes, there will be people doing similar things, unless your idea is totally unique (then well done you). The truth is though, most people aren't even in the game. People say they want to start up a business, leave their job, sell up and travel the world, start a band, etc. However only the brave few follow through with conviction and do it.

By the way, competition is good, it makes you raise your game to match or better your rivals and continuously improve.

Most people just dream it, wish it, or truth be told live their lives making excuses such as 'that's for other people who had a lucky break', or were born with rich parents, or had a different childhood or better education or different skin colour. They tell themselves every 'excuse' or 'lie' they can think of because make no mistake, it's hard-work stretching yourself beyond your current limitations. The thing is, it takes **time, energy, effort, commitment, blood, sweat and tears** to be an entrepreneur. If you truly commit to your project, business or idea (or any other challenge in your life for that matter), then you *will* succeed.

I was asked recently how I built my Training Centre, the person enquiring wanted to do 'something similar'. He'd seen me and my team succeed and thought we were making a fast buck. I even gave him the blueprint. When I told him of the hard work needed upfront, pitfalls, dedication and legalities he disappeared. I could tell him everything, but he was missing the passion, determination and commitment needed. These are the ingredients that cost nothing and don't require skill, but nothing happens without them.

Don't get me wrong here, if you go through some soul searching and find entrepreneurship or building a business isn't for you, that's fine, there's always another path, it doesn't make you a failure. I haven't met you, but as a fellow human being I care about what happens to you either way. If this journey doesn't serve you personally, in some way then maybe life has a more fulfilling destiny waiting for you elsewhere. And the information contained within these pages will also help you succeed in any other endeavour; the strategies and motivational tips are not confined to starting a business.

Opportunity is missed by most people because its dressed in overalls and looks like work.

'Thomas Edison'

Social Conditioning

I wanted to add something in this book to show you what a massive step you're taking here to even think about breaking away to be your own person. Simply thinking about this means that you have something burning inside of you that's screaming to break out.

Just as we are *conditioned* by certain fear triggers in our lives to exhibit the fight or flight process, or rather more accurately the Freeze, Fight or Flight. We are also conditioned throughout our lives in our behaviour. Whether is it by teachers, parents, even self-talk. This is the reason people stubbornly wait at red traffic lights like complete planks even when an ambulance is right behind them, sirens sounding and lights flashing. We have been conditioned to stop at red lights and it's hard to break that conditioning, for the most part it keeps us safe. Recognise the fear (that little voice that says you can't do this) and use it to drive you towards your goal intelligently with purpose. (Note I'm not advocating blindly jumping red lights here).

If you are familiar with Pavlov's famous experiment with dogs, you will know that he conditioned them to salivate by introducing a bell every time they were fed. In time, sure enough they started to salivate just from the sound of the bell with the expectation of food being introduced. The experiments were in fact a bit more gruesome, but for our purpose this explanation this will suffice.

Like 'dogs' we can be and are being conditioned. The first words we learn as children with any passion are 'No' and 'Don't'. (Often followed up by 'sit down' and 'shut up'). Mostly to keep us safe from ourselves because as children we have no fears and just dive into everything.

We start school and learn to associate the sound of the bell with start of class, then another to herald playtime, then another for home time. In between is a fire bell which they tell us to associate with danger and we must leave quickly, quietly and in an orderly fashion and meet at the designated point. Outside we hear different sounds for each of the emergency services, sometimes we don't even realise they are different.

When timeshare holidays were all the rage, they used to sit loads of people in a room and whenever someone signed up, they rang a loud bell of some kind to let 'everyone' know someone was buying, then opened the champagne and treated them like stars. This fed into something psychologists call 'social proof' making decisions easier for everyone else to go with when you see others doing it.

Advertisers use this process to condition us to feel good; even while selling us shit that's bad for us like cigarettes and alcohol. An ad may go something like this;

A lone cowboy sits by his campfire in Wyoming, surrounded by beautiful scenery, calming music and he's happily smoking his pipe. As the smoke billows across the countryside, a young, beautiful lady smells this aroma, gets on her horse and sets off in pursuit of the source. She finds her man and they disappear into his tent together (implying sex is about to happen).

He briefly pops his head back outside to grab his tobacco and gives the camera a cheeky wink as he shows the product, with a name like 'allure' or some other shit with a worse strapline like 'get more allure'. The truth is, tobacco makes your breath, clothes and house, stink. It turns off women, gives you cancer and kills you. But the seed is set and bypasses conscious thought by playing nice music and framing the scene.

Adverts for cosmetics are just as stupid. 'Now with added pentapeptides'. A new one sells now with added Hyaluronic acid. Nobody questions what the hell these are because they show someone in a white lab coat showing the product.

Is it any wonder (and ironic) that some people get used to, and feel comfortable with prison and the routine when 'conditioning' has led us to conform ever since the moment we were born? In prison, you don't have to assume responsibility, you are told when to get up, eat, exercise and go to bed, by the bell.

We're so traumatized nowadays with media spreading fear of litigation, reports of paedophiles, murderers and terrorists hiding around every corner waiting to pounce, news of thousands of immigrants 'racing through the streets' 'taking our jobs', CCTV on every wall because we're told that we are not safe. We are breeding a nation of risk averse children.

A sense of adventure built the country and a sense of fear is destroying it citizen by citizen. Only you my friend can stop the rot.

Break the chains

In certain parts of Asia where they use elephants for working, they 'condition' them, so they don't run away. How?

They chain the elephant's leg when the animals are young, and naturally with the exuberance of youth they tug and pull and fight with all their might to get free. Over time, although they grow bigger and stronger, the chains are not increased in strength. So why don't they escape? Because trying and failing while they were small cements the 'belief' in them that they can't escape. So, they stop trying.

We are no different, our belief in what is possible is taken from past-experience. Children are told don't do that, you'll get hurt, stop, you can't, you're too small. Remember, you were a different person when you were younger, and you now have a different mindset, different skills and greater cognitive abilities. It's time to break the chains, forget the labels that were placed on you by incompetent teachers and a peer group with no ambition, re-condition yourself, this is not my gift to you, it's your gift to yourself.

Incidentally it's also in school that unfortunately free thinking is considered disruptive rather than individual and an inquisitive mind. Imagine if Albert Einstein had asked his teachers at age 16 his famous thought "Sir, what would the world look like if I travelled on a beam of light?" the question that had a role leading to his special theory of relativity. My guess is he might have been told to shut up and stop disrupting the class and asking stupid questions.

No, my friend I am not a fan of school as you may have gathered, however I am a fan of 'education', of collecting and imparting useful knowledge. School didn't do it for me, why was I learning about Henry VIII? My thought was that 'there's no future in history'.

By the way, education is not intelligence. People often say they are not intelligent as they didn't attend school or attain great grades. Education is learning. Intelligence is putting what you have learned into beneficial practice. For instance, did you learn French at school? Yes, so now you go to France regularly and speak French like a native, don't you? What do you mean, no?

Schools will never change young people's lives by teaching a curriculum that is uninspiring and dull. Expecting every learner to fit into the constraints of a few subjects developed a century ago that have little relevance to them today. Then they call them uninterested, disruptive or stupid because they can't relate to the lessons. Some teachers teach kids the way I've seen Brits speak abroad. They speak in our foreign tongue to the locals and if they are not understood, they shout louder with a patronising tone because that works doesn't it. "Hola where's the toilet por favour? I said WHERE'S THE TOILET POR FAVOR? Stupid foreigner.

They don't speak the students' language, do they? Why don't they teach communication skills, finance, respect in relationships and self-respect? School tells us that we can, or we can't, your good at something or you're not, and it sets that belief forever. I'm telling you my friend that that's bull. We have different degrees of proficiency, but everything can be learned, practiced and improved. Yet people leave school believing they are no good at maths, or art or languages. Worse, some people leave school believing they are stupid. So sad.

I'm here to tell you that you don't have to be the best to be successful. Being the best is great (so they tell me) but guys, there's only one 'best', and it's a subjective point of view anyway. Over 7 billion people on earth and most of them doing something. While ever you are in the game, moving with intent, you will have some degree of success. Get out of the Pidgeon holes the school put you into, its bullshit. Take the life you really deserve.

Note to my younger self

This is a letter I wrote just for you
For the things in the future I wish that you knew

I know you'll have doubts cos life can be tough
Remember though that being yourself is enough

Teachers will say you're a dreamer, that's right
Cos you're a free thinker and it gives them a fright

They don't like being questioned, ideas or thought
'be seated, be quiet, just listen, be taught'

They'll constantly label you but how can they say
That you won't make your life successful some day

So, the next time they tell you that you 'cannot do'
It's their limitations and that's not for you

If they have all the answers and their lives are so great
Ask why they're still teaching children of eight.

Later in life you'll get a new boss
Who'll see you're exhausted and won't give a toss

And when you're successful though he gave you the sack
He'll be your best mate and jump on your back

Hold on to your dream it's there for the taking
In the recipe that we call life that your baking

So, one word of warning for when you've succeeded
Your friends were the ones who were there when you needed

Dave Brazer

Bullet proof mindset

During your time as an entrepreneur, you will need to be prepared for people who will try to talk you out of it (bosses, colleagues, even family), make no mistake about that. Not always because they don't like you, but because they see you leaving them behind and doing what they haven't the courage or commitment to do as you become more confident and focussed. These are the people that visit you in hospital, eat all the grapes and tell you about someone they know who 'died of that'. Positivity vampires.

Make no mistake, people will pull you down, but these people don't realise that everyone achieves success, the question is for whom. Winners achieve success by working hard and creating it from an idea, using whatever force they can. The people sitting at home watching Jeremy Kyle, munching Cheetos while scratching their balls and putting other's achievements down also achieve success, by driving the successful people who use other's negativity to propel themselves forward and resolve never to settle for the limitations afforded to their counterparts.

Successful people use positive and negative comments and events to drive themselves. People who don't take responsibility for their own destiny and try to convince themselves that success is down to luck are deluding themselves and selling themselves and the life they could have short.

Remember, trying to destroy a man's reputation with lies is like dousing yourself with cheap perfume. Everyone knows you stink before you open your mouth. In order to succeed you must surround yourself with people with the same values and people who will encourage and most of all challenge you.

Some people will tell you the idea is stupid, say it'll never work, tell you someone else tried and failed or tell you how you need to go out and get specific skills, talent or *qualifications before* you try, bull.

Do you remember the time you first had sex with the love of your life? While you were dragging each other's clothes off in the back of your dads Mk 4 Cortina, as her feet pressed up against the glass like two internal windscreen wipers, smudging the ever increasing condensation and you battled to stop your ass pipping the hooter, did you stop and say something like, "Alison what are we doing, I'm not qualified for this, I don't have a certificate. Is that what happened? Probably not, and if it did you probably *were* certified soon after but not in the same sense. Oh, and don't ask how I know her name was Alison!

Belief in yourself, your product or service is essential. If you believe in it after you've done your homework don't be swayed by people trying to put you off. You must have unbridled determination and focus *'until'* you get there. 'Until' is an important word to the entrepreneur and to anyone wishing to succeed.

Make no mistake, things will go horribly wrong and just as you think you've made it something else will come along to trip you up. But if it means something to you, do not quit. You need massive determination to start any business and carry on through adversity.

I was warned over and over that my business wouldn't work but I went ahead (remember I'm stubborn) we've since won numerous awards for the organisations, most recently from the Duke of York awards and we have won many contracts. Having said this, you also need to use intelligence. It's so easy to focus so much on proving the idea is good you can become blinkered to seeing what is working and not seeing what isn't.

"Be yourself, everyone else is taken"

Oscar Wilde

My business journey so far

It's easy to believe that entrepreneurs come up with a business idea, put it into action and become an overnight success. Usually, though not always, nothing can be further from the truth. They say on average, people try ten businesses before they crack it. Most successful entrepreneurs have worked through adversity and gone through numerous failures (lessons) before they eventually found the right business for them and gathered the necessary skills to carry the business forward.

Let me tell you about my early 'lessons' in business
I suppose my first foray into the world of business was with my mate at school, Mario. His uncle had a corner shop and one day we were in there when he was having a clear out. A large sweet jar caught our eyes. It didn't contain sweets though, it contained hundreds of scratch-cards. 'Maz' asked his uncle if we could have them if they were being thrown out. They were out of date by some years', so he agreed we could have them for a bit of fun. We weren't thinking about fun though, we were interested in profit.

We started to sell the cards at school and in our eyes, we were doing nothing wrong as we were paying winnings out when anyone won, so everyone was happy. Although our asses squeaked a bit when we walked, thinking someone may win the jackpot of £25000. Well, a few teachers soon got wind of this and we even sold some to them, making a right killing by the way, but one of the more severe ones caught us and we received an all-mighty bollocking from him and were consequently frog-marched to the headmaster. They muttered something about gambling laws and gaming rules in school which we didn't understand, (Our story and we we've stuck to it). That business ended abruptly for some reason, but more importantly it ended in the black.

We continued our partnership by making ginger beer, (just to drink at first) which entailed storing bottles in the airing cupboard. I have to say it tasted great, so we started to sell some. Then one day we started a new batch. We forgot about it though as you do when you are so young and have lots going on in life like chasing girls. I think we fermented it too long in the warm and the whole batch promptly exploded in the airing cupboard in Maz's house. His mum was not happy and was finding glass everywhere for years after that, and everything smelled of ginger (no jokes about Fred Astaire's fingers please).

My young life was filled with these ventures which were more opportunistic than planned, but they gave me the first desire to have my own business and a buzz that I never got working for other people. I was 12 when I first remember saying I want my own business and a Mercedes. We used to hang about outside in those days, interact with our friends rather than text all day (probably as we didn't have mobile phones), you know the kind of thing. This was in the days when you had to approach a girl you liked and talk to her to try your luck. And take the walk of shame back to your mates if she told you to piss off. Nowadays there are apps for that.

Well we used to hang around in a local dump among other places, there were all kinds of goodies to be found. One day, we found hundreds of razor blades, still packaged. I'd just started my first day at work at 16 (on dad's orders) and on telling my new colleagues, a bunch of hairy assed factory workers that I knew where to get razor blades I was shocked to find Brazer's Razors had a full order book by the end of the day. **A lesson there, everyone's junk is someone's gold.** That weekend we climbed into the dump and collected these blades that had been chucked away. I sold the lot. A great weekend out on the piss was our prize from the proceeds.

Monday morning wasn't so great though. My new workmates surrounded me and complained that the razors, in their words "wouldn't cut the hairs off our prick". I suppose "You should have told me that's what you wanted them for" was probably the wrong response, but at sixteen-years-old I thought it was witty at the time. Luckily the lads saw the funny side of it and didn't kick my ass.

Prestige Art
I heard that there were people in Taipei, Taiwan who would paint portraits from photographs, so I looked up the information, took a photograph of my girlfriend and sent it off with the money. Two weeks later a parcel turned up in a giant loo-roll, my girl's picture, painted on canvas. The likeness was good (and made a great dartboard after the divorce) but because I took the photo and wasn't a great photographer it was pretty two dimensional. Still, off I went, wandering around aimlessly showing the painting to people asking them to have paintings done of their loved ones. I even bumped into a famous snooker player in the lift at a hotel in Sheffield and asked if he wanted one doing. We had a nice chat, but I didn't secure a sale. Although I didn't know it at the time that was my first actual elevator pitch and not my best.

The trouble was, I had no strategy, no sales experience, no business cards and no idea about business. I had some limited success, but new machines which produced pictures on canvas from photos started appearing. This stopped my business in its tracks. I didn't really mind this as for me it was always a learning exercise. I did learn a lot though which would be useful in my business journey.

41

D-Tect Investigations
I had always fancied being a Private Investigator. Maybe spurred on by watching Magnum PI driving his red Ferrari and getting the girls. I didn't fancy wearing those tight shorts though, his voice was far too high for my liking and driving an open top Ford Capri in Yorkshire didn't have the same appeal as a Ferrari in Hawaii.

Anyway, I rented a crap office in an even worse area because that's where my work (and my budget was). The type of place where even the Alsatians had minders. Maybe it was because I couldn't join the police (and I believe there's always another way) or maybe it was the romantic notion of what a P.I did. Boy was I wrong. Yes, the job had its moments of excitement, but there was lots of research to do which bored me to tears. I didn't particularly enjoy working nights, getting attacked, being threatened or having idiots chasing me through the streets with knives either.

There were other parts of the job I loved though such as only having myself to rely on, this gave me a buzz knowing I had to deal with whatever came along. It's amazing though how much kicks off around you when you're trying to sink into the background. One night I was in a doorway outside a nightclub, merging into the background. Within seconds an altercation kicked off and a bunch of bouncers were laying into these guys within inches of me, worse was, my marks had left the club and I couldn't get to my car, I lost them.

The one thing that didn't suit me was delving into people's lives. I'm the least nosey person you'll ever meet, and unless

I'm helping them, I'm not really interested in what people get up to in their own lives, behind closed doors, that's their business, it doesn't affect me.

An Auntie, on the other hand could tell you what curtains everyone in the street had up, their wallpaper, where it came from, how much it costs and how long it's been up. What she didn't know about people wasn't worth knowing. She knew what everyone did for a living, even if they worked for MI5. She knew who was sleeping with who, on what day and where they met. All this before the invention of Facebook and without stepping foot past their front door. Years later she became known as Auntie 'Google'.

The day I stopped doing this job was after I'd been following someone at night for an investigation. My wife had called me briefly to have a nag (she would say discussion) about something or other (something about never listening to her) and I mistakenly told her where I was. She was a nurse and inherently worried about everything. Although I had driven off just after the lecture (sorry I mean conversation), she on the other hand admitted a guy into the High Dependency Unit where she worked who had been shot, on the street where I had been working. It wasn't until I returned in the morning that I realised she'd been worrying all night. I thought it best to move on from this job after the constant arguments that I didn't have any back-up, and nobody knew where I was (which wasn't really selling it to me that I should stop). I tried something safer after that.

Trance-Formation Hypnotherapy
I'd studied Therapeutic Hypnotherapy some years earlier, just because it interested me. However, I had just started a job in the community at the time which I really liked, so didn't run it as a business at the time. I decided that if I practised as a hypnotherapist, it was something I enjoyed, was relatively

good at. Anyway, I thought could also set up with zero costs other than getting business cards printed (then I could make the printer forget the fee).

Hypnosis is good for psychological issues, weight loss, IBS or stress related issues and sexual problems (In fact, I never had a problem getting sex since I started hypnotising the girls) JOKE!

I remember when I was training, I was confident enough to experiment. I once put my hypnosis partner 'under' and gave her the suggestion she was drinking a bottle of 'confidence' When I brought her around, she felt confident all right, but she was absolutely rat-arsed. I had to put her under again before the tutors saw her and put in the suggestion that when she awoke this time, she would be sober. That was an experience.

I had my first taste of using my new skills while still in my job. My colleague and I went on a visit in the community and found our clients mother had taken ill. We phoned an ambulance and decided to wait. The ambulance took hours and our clients' mother was getting more and more agitated. I used my hypnosis skills to calm her down and lower her heartrate which was beating out of her chest. You should have seen the look on my colleague's face when I started the Svengali routine, she thought I'd lost the bloody plot. She said later "I thought you were going to get her dancing around like a chicken or Elvis (a common misconception).

Word spread around work and a colleague Julie, the most sceptical person I ever met regarding hypnosis asked (Challenged) me to help her. She hadn't slept properly in about 7 years, since her son was born. I hypnotised her after work and she spent about half an hour 'under'. She slept incredibly well for 2 weeks and then started to drift back to her old sleep pattern and said I'd failed. I said hang on, you haven't had a good night sleep in 7 years, I spend half an hour with you which resulted in 2 great weeks sleep and I've failed? A course of treatment is often the best way to really make a difference. I still get asked about doing this years later.

Citadel Associates

I was proud to establish Citadel (A Social Enterprise) which I designed to support the most marginalised people in South Yorkshire to find employment, training and career support. Those who other companies couldn't help, had no dedicated provision for, and those who had come to the end of regular provision without success.

This was set up after managing a company for someone else for 5 years. I put my heart and soul into that company, but the directors decided to split the company and seconded me elsewhere while they did it. I'm a loyal person and if this hadn't happened maybe I'd have taken their company further. I felt pretty much let down as I'd had no backup of any kind since I took over as manager with 12 staff. We had 42 people, 4 offices and a shop when I left. As it went, they asked me back, but I'd already made up my mind that I was going alone. I remember the Director say, "but you've got no money" I said, "I know", he said, "but you've got no job" I said, "I know" He gave me 2 weeks to change my mind, I didn't.

Citadel was born and we developed many innovations and have supported 1000's of people with disabilities (physical and sensory, Learning Disabled, Mental Health), Ex-offenders, BME, long term unemployed, people with addictions and young people. We celebrated our 11th birthday this year. One innovation was Ignition.

Ignition Training Centre

I started Ignition in 2014, a garage fused with a Training Centre. I don't, or at least I didn't know a damn thing about garages. I had a few shocked faces staring back at me the day I said in the restaurant, "I'm going to open a garage". You're allowed to call McDonalds a restaurant in Rotherham. As soon as we opened Ignition, we began to get lots of opposition and still do. We then knew we were doing something right. Citadel and Ignition have since saved local services over £1000,000 since we opened. This business has caused me the most heartaches and the most pleasure in equal measure. We've been open 6 years when disaster struck (Adversity).

Unlimited Potential
I have spent over 16 years supporting the most marginalised people in society to move on in their lives. Unlimited Potential is a new company which is dedicated to supporting the self-starters in life. Those people who are dedicated to Self-Development and Entrepreneurship. The world is changing rapidly. Particularly the world of business and there are now greater opportunities to become wealthy than ever before. I want to help people explore the Psychological, Financial and Practical solutions to opportunity together.

Unlimited Potential helps those brave individuals who refuse to allow circumstance to control their lives. We do this through offering Self development tools, publications and workshops of our own and through a network of partners. We hope to see you on one of our events soon. Details to be found at Davebrazer.com. or unlimited-potential.org. This is where you invest in the most important thing in your life – YOU.

Our fathers and grandfathers had a certain idea of work. Get up at 3.30, walk 5 miles to work in bare feet do a 12-hour shift and walk home. Did they become financially independent? Not a chance.

We work 8 hours a day, what about the other 16 hours? To be financially independent we need to be earning 24 hours a day. The internet makes this possible, there are people out there

46

who prove it. If you wanted to earn £100,000 a year that equates to £273 per day, £11.00 per hour if you are earning 24 hours a day. The landscape is very different from the Business Studies course I did many years ago. More about this below.

Public Speakers College

Public Speakers College supports the development of public speaking and communication skills, from beginner to professional. We are in the information age and the art of public speaking has never been so important as it is today. From gaining a job through interview to giving a keynote speech or the presentation of your life. Public-speakers-college.org

This company incorporates SPEAK, **The Society of Practical Education and Knowledge**. A group of successful speakers, business people and imparters of knowledge make up the organisation and support us to deliver the training that helps make you as successful as they are, and they are available for hire as Keynote Speakers in their own right.

Send your details to me directly at DaveBrazer.com to be added to a database if you wish to attend any of the events or training and development days and invest in yourself.

People ask how I became an entrepreneur.

It was due to education!

I was patronised by demoralised and uninspiring teacher's, so I failed my exams and became an entrepreneur.

Dave Brazer

My Business Studies

I had made what I thought was an investment in myself and completed a business studies course at college some years before starting Prestige Art. I had always regretted not going in to do a degree, so I did this course to get a place at university and go into either further business studies or psychology, my other passion. I didn't do this as I had a much more precious gift arrive in my life, my daughter Lois. She was the catalyst I needed to finally get my entrepreneurial career started.

Anyway, this is when I began to realise that almost nothing, they taught in the Business Studies course had prepared me for business in the real world. To be fair to them, this was an access to Higher Education course as a prequal to going on to do a degree. These are the things we did in the course:

Business plans, yes you need a plan, but you need an idea first, college didn't go through business 'ideas' with us and how to make them happen. That, to me would have been a magnificent course. The old saying goes 'Those who can do and those who can't, teach. I'm not sure I believe that entirely, maybe more like 'those who teach have forgotten'. We never saw or wrote an actual business plan either, how strange.

Marketing, marketing what? Without a business what do you market? My marketing teacher was not the worst, but he was undoubtedly the most disillusioned tutor I have ever met. He obviously didn't want to be there and just gave us reams of paper to read each day. B.O.R.I.N.G. He then had the cheek to say in my report "I don't seem to remember David" Well I bet he remembered the wall clock he couldn't keep his eyes off. Rant over.

Stocks, and shares, This, was quite an interesting subject although not really needed unless that is what you are going to be doing in business. We followed stocks for a while in the paper to see if we made or lost money but that was it. I went to a conference recently and learned more about the stock market in half an hour than I did on the course. From a millionaire who's done it.

Politics, the favourite subject of our main tutor. He was a nice guy, but he taught a few subjects, but everything always came back to politics. Not that it wasn't interesting what he said but we wanted to know how to start a business, not why lobbying was called lobbying, or the history of Black Bob (ask my auntie Google). Again, nothing to do with starting a small business on a personal level. Of course, the political agenda shapes the world around us but again at the stage we were at, it didn't really enhance a course on Business studies.

Accounts, yes, Accounts are needed, of course but there are basic rules to follow and at the most basic, keep records of everything bought and sold. Try Quick-books if you have some IT or book keeping knowledge. Anyway, there are accountants for that, and they can save you a fortune in the end. Entrepreneurs don't want to be bogged down by such details (sometimes our downfall). Accounts are a good skill to have but it's a Marmite skill, you love it or hate it, and you don't really understand its intricacies in a practical world until you are running a business so for me it was an abstract art when I was 17 doing a Business Studies course. I found myself an accountant when I started Citadel and I still have the same accountant to this day.

Study Skills, These, lessons were all about ensuring we could research the information we needed for the course and reference where we found it. Don't get me wrong here, I don't believe any learning experience is lost. I merely think there could have been a better choice of curriculum for this part of our entrepreneurial or business journey, i.e. the very beginning.

I've since been on other courses which have been a real eye opener. I wish I'd been on these back in the day because I would be a millionaire 10 times over by now. And done the Social businesses on a larger scale. The only thing is that I had to pay for them, but they were more than worth it. Maybe there's a lesson there.

The only thing sadder than someone who can't, but tries,

Is someone who can, but won't

Dave Brazer

Dragon's Den

Have you ever watched Dragons den? A TV program where entrepreneurs go into ask a panel of multi-millionaires for investment in their business idea. At times it transpires that they have already pumped in hundreds of thousands of pounds into their (sometimes lunatic) idea.

"Hello Dragons, I'm the inventor of the world's first 3D printed parachute. I'm looking for £100,000 investment for 5% of my business. PLEASE DON'T DO THAT, this is called insanity. After these revelations it takes the Dragons seconds to tear the entrepreneurs apart. If you go onto this show, be thoroughly prepared. What I can't understand is where do they get this kind of money to throw away on a project, idea, invention in the first place. We don't want to become like a moth banging our heads on the same window for days on end. Find an open window.

The Knockers
No not those knockers. The kind of person who puts you down. People who put their head above the parapet will always have others who try to belittle them, put them down, discredit them or downright mock them. The reason is that these people either see you doing something they want to do, being like they want to be or getting something that they want to have but haven't the guts to get it.

They are the people who take the piss when someone gets up to sing at Karaoke at the local pup, laugh, heckle and joke to their mates about the state of him, the 'who does he think he is' brigade. Thing is they may very well be a better singer, but who got up? It is probably their confidence Mr Piss take is jealous of, or their sense of freedom.

Question, have you ever watched Britain's got talent? They don't do it so much now but in the early days the focus was on the people who thought they could sing but really (I mean really) couldn't. On one memorable occasion; an awkward, nervous and slightly dishevelled lady walked on stage, the groans and laughs were immediate and audible. The judges whispered profanities about her to each other. Who do you want to be like? asked Simon Cowell. "Elaine Paige", she exclaimed, and everyone laughed uncontrollably.

With the laughter ringing in her ears, she started to sing. The shock in everyone's faces was a picture. This incredible voice started to project, "I dreamed a dream of days gone by", from Les Misérables, and suddenly the laughter stopped and turned into utter amazement. Susan Boyle was her name and through what everyone else thought was impossible, in those two minutes she changed her life forever. Laughter turned to cheers, which turned to a standing ovation. Susan is now worth an estimated £12 million. Simon has since said that he was disgusted in himself and his initial reaction to seeing Susan walk on stage. She changed that program forever too.

You may also go through disbelief on your way up. Have no fear, once you begin to fly, their laughter gets impossible to hear anymore. And even of you do hear it, you won't care by then. People who put you down are already way below you.

Ask yourself on a regular basis "Is what I'm doing working"? and be prepared to change your approach to get results. This will save you hitting your head against that window just to prove a point. A word here about work life balance. I tend to get fixated on getting something done but neglect home life or downtime. Learn by my mistake and give yourself and your family/friends part of your time. They are who you work for.

You will be re-energised for this. Rewarding yourself for small successes keeps you motivated and able to carry on.

Adversity

Adversity, some call it '**Master**' **some call it 'Teacher'**. It depends on what you want to be, Student or Slave. As Clint Eastwood, might say, "Bad days are like assholes, everybody has them" As sure as you have a hole in your jacksie, you will encounter adversity, yes you will. We all have bad times, we all hate them and if we're smart, we all learn something as we get through them. This is an understatement if ever I said one.

The more you put your heart and soul into your business, the more it has potential to rock you to the core when the proverbial hits the fan. When my Training Centre burned to the ground. It was the second most heart wrenching time of my life. I felt like giving in. Actually, I felt like dying inside. More on this below.

We can do everything in our power to prevent terrible things happening (business planning, financial planning, training, prayer, etc.) but nothing will stop you having 'one of those days, weeks, years' from time to time, and because you're an entrepreneur you are probably, like me, hard on yourself. That's our nature to make things happen and control the situation we are in. Sometimes though, just sometimes, we must roll with the punches and take it on the chin. 'Down' doesn't mean 'out'. We can always as the song says get up, dust ourselves down and start all over again. It really is hard to stay motivated sometimes, but this is where your beliefs and your support network comes in. Whether it is your partner, friend, mentor or business partner.

Sometimes, you need to adopt a boxer's mindset. When life's throwing everything at you it's sometimes better not to mix it, take a step back to see what's happening, hang on and ride out

54

the storm if your legs have gone then wait and unleash your best punches when the time's right and you can see the target.

Adversity is part of life. It's how you deal with it that counts. If something doesn't cause you injury, or the situation won't kill you then it probably isn't as bad as you think. Some people just can't handle major stress, such as their local Barista forgetting the fancy design on top of their cappuccino. So, if your cheese dip fell on your suit before an important meeting don't sweat it, life will go on. If you think 'I bet we'll look back on this and laugh one day', why wait for one day in the future to laugh? Tell them in the meeting if you fell on your ass and have a laugh about it there, it might break the ice.

Believe it or not, adversity is a human need. Only through problems can you create solutions. Only by stumbling can we learn to walk, then run. A better quality of problem is your ticket to a better quality of life. This is the route to individual growth, it's how we grow as a team, a family, a nation and indeed as a species.

My advice for the bad days is to look back and see how far you have come since you began this journey. It really puts things into perspective. Look at your achievements and the list of things that drive you. Never forget your driving force as it is the fuel cell that will keep you going through the hard-times.

Remember, the sun doesn't really go down, it just shines on someone else for a while.

Mike Tyson - "Everyone has a plan until they get punched in the mouth".

A Secret to life:

"All you can do is *all you can do*, and all you can do is enough"

Art Williams

My Adversity Story

As I've already eluded to. Recently I lost my business as one Saturday night it burned to the ground. The business is a Training Centre called Ignition (must have been a premonition). Well I say I lost the business, I lost the place of business. At the time it felt like the same thing for me.

The scene was unbearable, utterly burned down and I'd just spent around £70K building the new Centre. In the window I could see my office wall. I had a poster on it, one of my favourite sayings from Winston Churchill, "If you're going through hell, keep going" The ceiling had been burned and was half hanging down. My good friend Ian saw it first through the window. The only part still visible was '**Keep Going**'. By Monday morning I had decided to fight for the business and one month to the day I had re-established the business elsewhere. I'm only telling you this to highlight that these strategies work, at least for me.

These are the times you must dig deeper than you realise you are capable of. This is when you must remember your 'reason' your 'Why' or find a new one. The passionate reason you went through this in the first place or you will give in. This relates to more than business, it's about anything you are passionate about and face loss. Relationship, job, money, house, you get the idea. One day instead of freaking out when you're out of milk, you realise you are handling the big stuff that would have phased you before.

Thing is, for a long time before the fire, I had been feeling that I didn't want to carry on with this business. I had new ideas and my passion is getting things started not running it for 5 years. This is something I think most entrepreneurs go through, they get bored whenever things stop being a challenge. I was getting bogged down by contracts and tenders, bid writing and day to day drudgery of business. I had moved 4 times through different issues and started again each time, but this time felt like the end. I was completely devastated but I remembered my default belief that I never quit, I suppose the fire gave me another challenge, so I set about starting again.

I have to say though that my recent passion about supporting entrepreneurs like you is really taking hold of my imagination now and although I have begun planning to start 2 more Ignition Training Centres, Unlimited Potential and the Public Speakers College are where I am focusing my energies this year. This has however increased my self-belief that I can do them all but can do and want to do are two separate things. My team will have the opportunity to take over if things go well.

I'm not going to go into this but there have been some significant other issues in my life the past year too. The reason I say this is to prepare you that when the shit hits the fan it really hits. I've been told many times last year that I'm inspirational due to overcoming all of this, but the reality is I'm just a normal guy who refused to give in. That's all, just carry on because the alternative is don't carry on and it's important to me that I show my partner that I'll always fight for her and show my daughter that there is always a way through adversity.

There's no denying that life can be a beach, there you are one day walking through the sand and the next you tread the same path and stand on glass with one foot, donkey poo with the other and while you're on your ass you see a tsunami heading your way. But when you think about it you wouldn't want it any other way.

Adversity doesn't get easier, and it certainly doesn't stop once you reach a certain age. In fact when you put your head above the parapet you could be in for more, but you just become better at handling it and there comes a time in your life that you realise you've been through so much that you'll get through next time cos anyone can do 'easy' and you're not just anyone.

This is the paradox that we face. We don't want adversity in our lives but the more adversity we face, if we can get through it, makes us stronger than we were before. This goes for other things such as loss, pain, rejection, embarrassment, fear and other so-called negative emotions. All the rewards are found on the other side of these emotions. Let's look at these in more detail.

I thought about giving up

Then I gave up,

I gave up thinking about giving up

Dave Brazer

All emotions are positive

Fear
Will Smith, the Fresh Prince himself tells a story about the time he and his drunken friends decided to do a sky dive. As he relives the moment, he wakes up the next morning and slowly remembers what they have all decided and as he recounts the fear in the pit of his stomach the audience are in stitches. He goes on to tell about the moment he meets his friends again the next day, hoping they have 'forgotten' the pact, then realises they are still up for it (or nobody wants to be seen to back out). So off they go to do the skydive.

He recalls how he felt with a guy strapped to his back (not something most guys are comfortable with) and making small talk while watching the traffic light system on board that tells you when to jump. He then suddenly realises that this is the first time he's been in a plane in which they open the door in mid-air. The lights turn to green and he watches his mates shuffle along the plane strapped onto their instructors. Then he reaches the edge, looking down, he's told they will jump on the count of 3, and on 2 he's shoved out in case he grips onto the side.

He then realises that the moment after jumping out and after the initial fright is the most serine and fantastic moment where you feel like you are flying. He also asks, "what was the point of worrying the night before, or in the van", before the flight. Everything worth anything to us is just on the other side of fear (remember Adam Peaty). Go for it.

Loss

Loss is one of the most significant things we must deal with in life, especially when it involves the loss of a loved one. Usually the first experience we have of loss is of a pet, then a friend as we leave schools or move up classes. Divorce is another loss akin to a bereavement and of course bereavement itself. The later in our life we deal with loss and the more protected we are it seems, the harder it is to tackle. Some of the greatest entrepreneurs have lost everything, businesses, fortunes, marriages, but somehow, they come back and create new businesses, rebuild fortunes and remarry. One you have something, it is in your psyche that it is possible, and it is therefore easier to get back again. This is a fundamental reality of psychology. If you believe it is possible, then it is.

Embarrassment

Everyone gets embarrassed, the more you can combat embarrassment, the easier your life will be. Did you ever see the hilarious movie, 'See no Evil Hear no Evil? Gene Wilders character, 'Dave Lyons' is deaf, and Richard Pryor plays the character 'Wally', a blind man. The movie follows the pair as they get embroiled with a gang and the police both chasing them after a murder at their news stand.

In one scene, Wally and Dave are chatting in the park, eating ice-creams. Dave Wally asks, "what do you want out of life"? and Dave say's "I guess not to make a fool out of myself". He says he's always had a fear that he's going to make a mistake and everyone's going to stand around and stare at him. Wally says, "I wish I'd have met you 8 years ago, I can fix all your problems in 10 seconds". Dave says, "oh yeah, 10 seconds eh" and Wally says "yes if you trust me" Dave agrees, and Wally sticks his ice-cream on Dave's head. He asks "how does that feel? You look a little silly to me". Dave is initially annoyed but then laughs as he realises what Wally has done, taken away that fear. Wally says, "you see, life isn't so complicated".

We are all fearful of so many things that in our mind are insurmountable, imaginary fears of something that sometimes debilitate us to the point of not enjoying the very thing that could be our talent or enrich our life. But at the end of the day it doesn't matter what people think of us, it matters what we think of ourselves. So, the next time something embarrasses you, don't let it rule you, its temporary, and forget about the past embarrassments. The past does not equal the present and the present is the start of your new future.

Pain
What is pain for. It is a mechanism to teach us what is dangerous or tell us there is something wrong. What's the first thing a Doctor asks, is there any pain, where, what kind of pain, it tells him a lot for a diagnosis.

We need pain. Pain immediately tells our nervous system that this will cause us harm unless we move our hand away. Emotional pain is similar, it tells us something is wrong in our life and we need to change it. We need pain and every emotion; even negative ones tell us something. Listen to the dis-ease you are feeling and move away from the situation.

The Myth of Failure

Entrepreneurs know instinctively that failure is part of success. In fact, it's a pre-requisite. Failing is learning – Success is putting that learning into practice in a positive way.

Failure and success are often just one step apart. Winners take that final steps to glory while quitters could so easily have succeeded but for one more try. Instead of beating yourself up when you feel that you have failed, embrace failure as an inevitable part of gaining the experience and resilience you will need to learn and grow.

Most of us have a deep fear of failure, especially in the eyes of people we love the most. True failure is giving up trying to be the best you can be. Failure is vital, if you are not failing you are not moving. Be sure to measure yourself against your own standards and expectations, not what others expect of you. Unless they expect the best of course.

I remember that my heart was in my mouth the day my daughter surprised me by climbing the stairs the first time, following me up there, she couldn't even walk. She stumbled at the top and slid all the way back down again. One of those moments when your heart stops, and you can't do anything but watch. She got back up then, and she has carried on getting back up ever since. Kids don't stop to ponder the concept of failure, do they? They just get back up and move forward time after time (**Magic Success formula).**

Entrepreneurs who failed
Every great Entrepreneur has failed at one point and will also continue to fail occasionally in their life. They dare to fail and therefore they are destined to succeed. Failing is what makes Entrepreneurs successful and none have walked this journey without the companion we sometimes call failure.

Akio Morita SONY

Akio went out of his way to get mimeograph paper, cut it into strips with razor blades, and scrapped up enough metal for Sony's first ever tape recorder. Sony designed the first transistor-based radio. Eager to make Sony an international company, Akio looked for a way to sell the radios in America. Akio found a distributor who was down to sell the radio under Sony's name, and Americans loved it. Sony became an international company.

The profit from Sony's debut allowed the company to move on, and develop more innovative electronics, like an 8-inch television, and a video-tape recorder. After moving to America, Akio noticed that Americans loved music. He was surprised that they'd carry boom boxes around. So, he designed and manufactured Sony's best and most popular device. No one had ever thought of a portable cassette player before! The Walkman was an incredible success. Over 200 million copies were sold in the USA alone.

His first product however was a rice cooker that kept burning rice.

Bill Gates   Microsoft

Bill Gates in the early 1970's, before Microsoft, Bill Gates and Paul Allen started a company called Traf-O-Data. It was a traffic analytical company that read data and created reports for engineers based on roads/highways. Paul Allen quoted that between 1974–1980 Traf-O-Data had total losses of $3494 and they ended up shutting it down. However, that failure is what gave Bill Gates the experience and understanding in business that made Microsoft such as success (and made him the world's richest man). Had Bill Gates not experienced that failing prior, Microsoft would most likely never had been the success that it was.

Colonel Sanders   KFC

Surprisingly, the Colonel's famous secret chicken recipe was rejected 1,009 times before a restaurant accepted it. He founded Kentucky Fried Chicken when he retired at 65 years old. Colonel Sanders said "I only had 2 rules, 1 Do all you can and 2 Do it the best you can"

By 1964, Colonel Harland Sanders had 600 franchises selling his trademark chicken. Then, he sold his company for $2 million dollars but remained as a spokesperson. In 1976, the Colonel was ranked as the world's second most recognizable celebrity. It's an amazing achievement how the man started at the age of 65, when most retire, and built a global empire out of fried chicken. It's never too late to build your dream.

Henry Ford   Ford Motors

Known today as a business magnate, philanthropist and social entrepreneur, Henry Ford actually failed several times. His first two car companies failed and left him broke. But that didn't stop him from founding Ford Motor Company and become the first to apply assembly line manufacturing for cars.

He burned through all the money from his first group of investors without producing a car
He eventually produced a car and raised another $60,000 in share capital, but his Detroit Auto Company went bankrupt. In the 1920s, Henry Ford refused to update the Model T car, leading sales to fall dramatically. One of his mantras was "Failure is simply the opportunity to begin again, this time more intelligently."

This determination is one of the things that we find over and over in entrepreneurs and ensured that he became one of the three most famous and richest men in the world.

Richard Branson   Virgin
Even the fifth richest person in the U.K. didn't get to where he is now without a few failures along the way. Along with his famous Virgin Records and Virgin Airlines, he also developed Virgin Cola, Virgin Cars, Virgin Brides and Virgin Vodka. Haven't heard of them? That says it all.

Despite it all Richard Branson remains one of the biggest (known) successes in British business (I say known as there are many people you will not have heard of, but you will have bought their products or used their services) Richard is a philanthropist and his willingness to try over and over again is the hallmark of a great entrepreneur who has aimed for and reached the stars when he founded Virgin Galactic.

Soichiro Honda   Honda
Honda initially applied for a job at Toyota as an engineer but was turned down. Being jobless, he started making scooters at home, which he sold to neighbors. With the support of his family, he founded Honda, the world's largest motorcycle manufacturer. His first building burned down (something I can personally relate to), but he somehow carried on and established one of the most profitable automakers.

Thomas Edison   Inventor
Edison, one of the most prolific inventors in history (holding over 1000 U.S. patents), Some successful and others not so much. Entrepreneurs have this ability to move onto the next thing, failures are just lessons. Real failure is not trying at all.

Edison was told as a boy by his teacher that he was too stupid to learn anything and suggested he go into a field that did not require intelligence. Imagine if that teacher destroyed his motivation. We'd have been sitting in the dark today. He tried almost 10,000 experiments before he created the first light bulb, but he knew his outcome and worked 'until'.

Public Speaking

"No Way" I hear some of you shout, well unfortunately, or fortunately as the case may be, you may be asked to be a key note speaker, present a prize or speak at a gathering about your service or product at some stage as you become established. Even at base level, you are trying to sell your business or service to people. It would be remiss of me to ignore this topic and not give some guidance and include it in this book.

Of course, you will die if you speak publicly and mess up. No? so, would you collapse and end up being hospitalized? No, so will your wife leave you? will you lose your job, probably not as you are the boss! Obviously, I'm just joshing with you here to illustrate that there are much worse things in life than speaking to more than one person at a time. *That's all it is.*

While studying Hypnotherapy I first heard the statistic that in percentage terms, more people are afraid of public speaking than are afraid of dying. Well, to put this into context for you, people often speak at funerals, which would you prefer to be, the speaker or the deceased?

Everyone gets nervous when public speaking, this is entirely normal, and we've all messed up. Nerves are your body's way of getting the adrenaline pumping to get you ready for an activity. This adrenalin surge is what we *interpret* as nerves. It's the same process that moves you out of the way of an approaching car hurtling towards you. Another word for nervous is 'excited' so here are some thoughts on getting through.

Prepare Thoroughly

The more prepared you are the less nerves and anxiety you will suffer. Write your speech or presentation and learn it but don't get hung up on it if you miss a line when the time comes, the audience don't know what you are going to say. Write a signature speech that you know well that you can pull off at the drop of a hat. If you know your information and you know that you know the information that is half the battle.

Triggers

We all have triggers which make us stressed, but we can also have triggers that carry us through stressful times and it really depends on your personality type what will work for you.

Robbie Williams (not a shrinking violet) said in an interview that he suffers from stage fright. He combats this by being able to switch on something which tells him it's time to perform and the more nervous he feels the more brash and confident he comes across. He must have been seriously nervous at Knebworth, arguably his greatest performance.

Elvis Presley prepared himself with the music 2001: A Space Odyssey which filled the auditorium, as he walked the 1000 yards from his dressing room, the music built up into a crescendo, his trigger to forget the nerves and be 'The King'.

Picture This!

Some people advise that you should picture the audience naked as you speak. I don't know about you, but I found that when you are nervous about speaking in public (yes, it's happened to me too) then speaking to 50 naked people might send you into a state of sheer panic! I don't advise this at all. Hey, don't take my word for it, try it and see how you get on. But don't look down.

Props
Some people find props are good and it really depends on the speech or presentation you are giving. Please try to avoid juggling knives (not known for settling nerves) and avoid death by power-point like the plague. I was at a meeting about funding recently and the two presenters put up slides and proceeded to read them all word for miserable word (FOR TWO HOURS). If you do use this resource make the content simple to get the point across in a humorous way, use it as an aide memoir and fill in the blanks with your witty repartee. Otherwise people will get bored and cut into your presentation with their own thoughts or leave altogether.

Make it entertaining and memorable
People remember firsts, lasts, unusual things and humour. They also remember anecdotes (stories that relate to the topic) and analogies (This is like that) which put a point across that may be difficult to grasp or to add humour to a dull subject.

Check how you look
Remember to check your flies (preferably before you get to the stage). Particularly if you do try the above technique of picturing the audience naked. Otherwise if you see someone you find particularly attractive, they may get to see a prop none of you bargained for. At least the presentation won't be boring and would certainly be entertaining and memorable.

Ladies you also need to check your appearance. It's all very well looking glamourous, but it won't settle your nerves if you've tucked your skirt into your knickers whilst at the loo. Who can forget Richard and Judy of 'This Morning' presenting an award at the Brit awards 2000 where Judy Finnegan's blouse revealed more than the award winner? John Leslie running from the audience to cover her up (and get a closer look).

'Remember' Everyone gets it wrong sometimes

If you ever seen some of George Bush's speeches, you will see that you are not the only one who gets nervous or tongue tied. President Bush made some howlers in his time. Who could forget the speech in which he said "Our enemies are innovative and resourceful, so are we, they never stop thinking about new-ways to harm our country, and our people, and neither do we" In another speech, he said "I'm honoured to shake the hand of a brave Iraqi citizen who had his hand cut off by Saddam Hussein."

Bob Monkhouse once told the story of the 'Thick family' (of whom they changed the name for the show) 'Family Fortunes'. In this game-show the general-public had been asked a series of questions *prior to the show* and the family had to guess the top 5 answers given. Bob said, "We asked one hundred people to 'name something pink' and the lady who was the spokeswoman for the Thick family said "Is it my cardigan?

We aren't 'really' afraid of 'speaking' are we, we do it all day, every day. We are afraid of messing up and people laughing at us. Thinking about it though, aren't the best speakers the ones who make us laugh? It's worth having a few throwaway quips up your sleeve (not literally, people will see you reading your sleeve) to break up any nervous moments and get you back on track. A word here about telling jokes or 'one-liners' make sure you are comfortable delivering them. If they work and the audience laughs it really helps you settle down but if you are uncomfortable delivering this type of speech the jokes could be lost on your audience. Imagine Peter Kaye and Jack Dee delivering the same joke! Only you know which delivery style is closest to yours and the content of your speech.

71

FBI - "Proper Planning Prevents Particularly Poor Performance"

It's a good idea to get something prepared before you are even asked to stand up in public and speak. When you have something in reserve it's so much easier to write and learn the words under less stressful times and sometimes you may be put 'on the spot' and asked to say something about your company by a well-meaning person. This is so much easier if you have already planned something 'witty and funny'. You don't think that all the improvised quips from comedians on panel shows are really 'improvised' do you. I'm sure some are but no, they have a stock of one liner's which they can fit to any number of scenarios.

So, think about the purpose of your presentation. Whatever its purpose, it's up to you to engage with the audience and capture their attention, preferably within the first minute. Use a prop if you feel it enhances the presentation, engage fully with your audience, ask them questions if possible, captivate their attention with emotion and a story. Change your pitch, tone, timber and tempo to keep them focused on your voice, and **Finally - Enjoy the limelight, you have earned it.** Remember that if you are in the position of delivering a speech or presentation then it's because you have earned that position. Love it and enjoy the ride.

'Tip' Bob Monkhouse wrote a great book about public speaking – Complete speaker's handbook

"People laughed when I said I wanted to be a comedian, ha, they're not laughing now"

Bob Monkhouse

Battle of the sexes

Gentlemen, does your wife ever complain at you for flicking over the TV and channel hopping? Ladies, men do this because they don't want to know what's on, they want to know 'what else' is on. Even if they're enjoying the program that they are bloody watching. It's the old grass is greener on the other side complex even when we're sitting on our ass watching television. Men are impatient and they hate to watch adverts when there could be something else to watch. Entrepreneurs it seems need to keep looking at new things, especially when the old things get boring (I'm not talking about wives here).

Ladies, does your man complain that when you're shopping for dresses and you constantly pick up the dresses you don't like and try them on even though you know you don't like it in the first place? We scan a shop from the doorway and don't understand that you want to touch, look at and feel the clothes and that it's an experience for you. I say man by the way because once you've reached the marital status most men have learned to stay away from the missus asking their opinion on dresses, because she's already made up her mind that they like it before asking him. Not smart if he says no. Then there's the more toxic question about her bum looking big.

We are different in our approach, but they are not right or wrong, good or bad, just different and it's a lesson we can use to ensure we take a step back from time to time and look at things from fresh perspectives. If things are not going well, imagine how a business hero of yours would handle the situation. Imagine how a child would see it, or, ask the team their opinion. It isn't weak to ask. Entrepreneurs are often alone so reach out.

This is just a bit of fun, but it just highlights the fact that men and women sometimes have a different viewpoint. This is good news in business because it gives new insights into the business, not just different sexes but diversity in general. Guys seem to be focussed on one thing and can get obsessed until it is done. They can multi task but in general zoom in on something and chase it. Ladies tend to be better organisers, peacemakers and speakers. Pooling our, knowledge, resources, experience and ideas can be a magnificent way to create solutions to business problems and really take off.

By the way, the answer to the age-old question; we don't put the toilet seat down because we'd piss all over it if we did. Then you'd be really hacked off at us.

And guys, they go to the loo together to talk about you!

Women always worry about
the things that men forget

Men always worry about the
things that women remember

Albert Einstein

Focus on the task

Have you ever come home late, knowing your partner is in bed asleep and you don't want to wake her? So, you try to open the door as quietly as you can and make a complete hash of it. You try the wrong key, drop the keys in the pissing rain and dark, you've always got bags in your arms at these times, haven't you? Even if you never carry a bag. Then you fall in through the door (cos you forget the step that has been there for 15 years).

Inside, you scramble round for the light, (cos you've never located these before either have you). Then finally you walk upstairs with the lights off, carrying your shoes, and inevitably you drop one (a shoe) which magically turns into a bowling ball and bounces on every single step, hitting the door at the bottom. Even though gravity seems to have doubled, you still think you have been quiet as a mouse. She in the meantime has heard every crash bang wallop, chuntering and swearing and is sitting up in bed, arms crossed when you finally make it to the bedroom. What's happened, assuming you weren't pissed.

You were focussing on every movement, every step and missing the flow of just doing what is easy. This is what it is like when you try to walk on the ice and tense your body. It gets harder to walk.

Business is a bit like this; the more you try to control every single step, the more events control you. Put systems and people in place as soon as you possibly can. Concentrate on the bigger picture, let your team deal with the small things. I'm not saying take your eye off the ball here, that's insane.

I'm talking about making the most of the resources you have around you, be it people, finances, systems or support. Try to fit it all in yourself and taking control of everything rather than the important things brings you stress, that's when you stop seeing the metaphorical doorstep, key hole, lights and stairs right in front of you. Then you end up spinning plates, and that isn't what you started in business for.

Strategy
Near the start of this book I said that it's important to just take the first step. In fact, I put high importance on just doing it. On the face of it, what I'm about to say is in direct contradiction to that. Having a strategy is important to move the idea forward. So why can't we just start Dave, I hear you ask. Well you can if you know what you're doing 'go ahead'. I just go ahead even when I don't know what I'm doing sometimes, hence the mechanic Training Centre. I did however have a 10-year track record and therefore some essential skills before taking on this venture. So, the answer is yes you can just dive in if the time and the situation is right.

What if though you had a proper strategy to build your business. Wouldn't a plan of action be a better place to start from? This way, you know you are not going to miss anything out and you can be sure you do things in the correct sequence. You won't have to think about every single step if it is in a plan. The first step I previously mentioned could be to build a plan. When you telephone someone, you don't just punch a bunch of random numbers into the phone. It must be the right set of numbers in the correct sequence (syntax), including the area code if they are out of your area. Have a plan, a strategy and this is the equivalent of having your friends' numbers on speed dial.

You could build a house without plans, but would you? Plan as much as you can but be aware that those plans will change so be flexible and retain an awareness of how your plans play out. This way you get the best of both worlds and have the best chance of success.

Business planning

I don't want to get too bogged down by the process of business plans. Remember, this book isn't specifically written as a 'how to' book but I should mention some thoughts on the subject. There are millions of businesses out there and even more fantastic ideas. Having the determination to succeed is all well and good, in fact essential. If you want to be taken seriously by customers, funders, backers, banks or support organisations you should have a decent business plan. In other words, a strategy for your vision of the business and how you plan to take the idea forward. A good business plan will identify the business idea, give you an indication of where you are now in terms of your business acumen, potential pitfalls and competition, costs, your USP (unique selling point) and show you the barriers you need to overcome to get the idea off the ground.

You will be asked for your business plan if you are asking for help from the above organisations if you are developing a new idea. Having said this, don't get hung up on building a business plan, there are plenty of examples out there with useful headings. Just put your plans down on paper and you'll be surprised how it comes together. So, don't get too worried about this because it will come once you start to write it.

You know the business and the way it will work but please do write it down because as you read the business plan, or any other plans you have in life, it will form part of your reality in your own mind, and the mind doesn't discriminate between real and imaginary, that's why you become the person you think about becoming as long as you start taking action towards being that person and vividly imagining being there. No going back.

There are specific things you need to put in your business plan and lots of help out there to do it (Try the Chamber of Commerce) or the Prince's Trust have quite a comprehensive plan but it's a good idea when writing it to have Kipling's 6 honest serving-men in mind when thinking what you want to say (below).

So, the questions above show you the reasons for what you are doing and the strategy for doing so but you must never lose track of the end goal. Your 'Why' This is what drives you forward.

SWOT Analysis
I know you've heard this one before and it's a bit antiquated these days, but it still has some value. For those of you who haven't heard this term it stands for Strengths, Weaknesses, Opportunities, Threats. There are several variations, but it may be worth spending some time looking at these particularly if you are going to ask for financial help to start. Just like being back at school, a bank manager will have expected that you have done your homework. Lots of Business plans have these SWOTS incorporated. It's to get you thinking about your business from a more logical point of view because it's all too easy to get stuck in the middle of things when you are excited about your new venture.

Now, the details of your plan are going to be different from the next person, but I recommend that you should start with your 'Why' as afore mentioned. The reason you are in this, the end goal. Then everything else is just the steps the who, what, where and how. Make the plan compelling and exciting to you and make your story interesting to other people who may wish to support you.

You're the author of your own life and when you build a business it becomes an integral part of your story, of your identity. Make sure you get your message right.

Do you remember the guy in Australia who put an ad in the paper to sell his house, and they put No Asians in the advert? It caused a media storm and a journalist went to interview him. Asking why he didn't want Asians the man said because I don't like them, they are nothing but crooks. The interviewer said don't you know there are discrimination laws about what you're doing. Then it transpired that the ad should have said no 'Agents'.

"I keep six honest serving-men,

(They taught me all I knew);

Their names are What and Why and When and How and Where and Who"

'Rudyard Kipling'

Networking – Building your winning team

I'm not talking about walking round business events here, swapping business cards and throwing them in a box 'just in case they become useful'. It never ceases to amaze me how many events I've attended, spoken to potential clients and found synergy in our businesses, swapped cards and followed up with potential opportunities only to have emails and calls unanswered. That's something else psychologists refer to as *'insanity'*.

Why waste your valuable time (cost it up) and energy to attend networking meetings, collect numbers of people and not call them? This reminds me of the people that friend request anyone and everyone on social media even though they don't even know them. They have hundreds of 'friends' but only actually *know* 4 people…. It also happens on Linked-in and sites like this, I've had requests from people who work in other fields, nothing to do with my business who live abroad and will never meet me. Now I don't mind this, but it can detract from the people who could be making a real difference to your business.

It can be awkward when you know someone is just being polite and although they instigate the conversation and ask for your details have no intention of calling you. So, have some fun when you meet someone, and they say to you "we must get together soon", just try making a definite date and you'll see moves like you've never seen in your life if they were insincere as they make excuses about how busy they are, their cats just died, they're having an operation for gout or they're going to Shanghai on a business trip. Even worse on the flip side, has anyone said to you "you must call round some time" and have you appeared at their doorstep sometime later 'suitcase in one hand', toothbrush in the other. Develop relationships, however, don't waste time on people who waste your time. And make it a rule never to waste their valuable time either.

Real networking is about developing relationships with people with whom you can have a symbiotic relationship. If you belong to the fabled radio station WII FM (What's in it for me) you will lose out on the chance to give first which opens-up greater opportunities in the long run. When someone does something for us, we tend to want to reciprocate and help them back, and its often disproportionate.

By building your networks I'm talking about building long lasting, mutually beneficial working relationships. None of us can do everything ourselves, I know, I've tried it and its hard-work. You will (hopefully) get to a point where relying on other people is necessary, essential even and without a network it's impossible to grow beyond a certain point.

Tip: Don't expect anyone to have your back when it's against the wall, it's too tight a spot. When you are on your uppers, only the hardy few will stand by you. If you find people who do, hold onto them.

Remember this though! People remember your promises and respect your actions.

Only invite those people along for the ride, who are also prepared to help you push.

Confidence assertiveness

It can be a soul destroying and confidence depleting time when you are an entrepreneur, particularly in the early days. Confidence, contrary to belief, isn't fixed, it ebbs and flows for a million reasons. Of course, people consider themselves generally either confident or not, but it is usually situation based i.e. you may be confident driver but not so with the written word, or confident swimmer but not so with cross country running. By the way, don't be fooled into feeling insecure among people of higher status. The higher they climb the more insecure they become. Proficiency in any task brings confidence and the more you work at something the more proficient you get. Think back to the time you learned to drive. How you felt having to think of every movement in minute detail as you learned each skill and how your confidence grew as you picked up the skills necessary not only to move the car but to gain road sense and 'unconscious competence'.

Leadership

Leading a team can be the most stressful part of business for an entrepreneur. To you, the business is your life, the very heart of you. You have sweated blood to build the business and probably for the most part, alone. Then as the business grows you will need to employ staff. That's where your heartaches begin. The people who work for you will 'never' have the passion and commitment to the business that you do. Unless that is you choose people not only for skills but for passion in what you do. Choose wisely my friend, skills are obviously important but so is commitment and a passion to be the best. This way though you will lose staff as they go onto bigger and better things but that's a good thing as the business dynamic changes as new people arrive.

I have known managers who only employ the people they think they can manipulate or 'boss around', they are usually in middle management positions with some degree of autonomy, have autocratic style and power has usually gone to their head. The trouble is that in time (usually when it's too late) they find they have filled the place with people who are 'denying a village somewhere of an idiot'. Then when something has gone catastrophically wrong, they find themselves chasing their tails having to deal with it.

Remember anyone can lead an Ass. Leading people with opinions is harder but much more worthwhile in terms of ideas and reputation for the business. Having a formidable team behind you doesn't mean you are weaker, it means you are stronger. Who would want to be the head lemming Jumping off the cliff edge with the other lemmings following blindly?

Please ensure that when you start to employ people, they have the passion for the work in them or at least buy into your vision. Success is a team endeavour and only a team which buys into the organisation endeavour to develop the success of your company will help it succeed. Appreciate your team - In the words of 'Celine Dion' "Tell him, tell him that the sun and moon rise in his eyes, reach out to him. OK I know that's complete overkill, particularly if you are a guy managing a building company, but you get the idea. Letting your team know that they are appreciated is as important as every other aspect of the business, probably more so. Your team includes your networks, friends, family, customers, funders (contractors) and staff.

80% of success is showing up

20% is following up

Woody Allen

Misfits

If you are different, if you stand out – That's your cue to be 'Outstanding'

Misfits often make great entrepreneurs. It seems that the more challenging your upbringing the more entrepreneurial you become. Trust me, I wasn't deemed the smartest kid in school (as my aunty reminded me recently).

I don't ever remember really 'fitting in' or feeling 'this is where I belong'. As I had epilepsy, I was the quiet kid who didn't show an opinion so people thought I had none. Strange how the quieter people often have more to say than people who shout. I did, however, have a burning need inside me to change my life, but I didn't know what I wanted to change or how to do it. I wasn't unhappy but not content with my lot either. Maybe part of it was an 'I'll show them' attitude when teachers who should have inspired all of us, instead tried to humiliate the ones who didn't conform to their view of the world.

As I grew older, I wanted something more than the prospect of living in one place all my life as other people seemed content to do, sometime on the same street, in the same house. Or working for the same company till I dropped down dead. Or as previously mentioned, going to the same pub with the same people having the same conversations and moaning about the same issues that they had decided to live with or decided not to change (the same thing in my opinion).

Misfit entrepreneurs forsake the safety of conformity to stand in the firing line to be ridiculed by lesser minds, and they dare to ask the bigger questions and bold statements. Statements like there must be something better than this product, service or idea, and if they discover that there isn't, they create something better. Misfits are innovators.

Innovation, invariably, one man strives for it, hundreds mock him for it and thousands benefit from it. That's the moment the idiot becomes an entrepreneur.

If you are different from the crowd, that difference could be the very thing that brings you incredible success. Be proud of, and true to who you are and put your head above the parapet. If you are somewhat of a misfit, you will no doubt be used to criticism. Take from life what you are worth. It doesn't come easy but guess what?

Anyone can do 'easy'.

Practicalities

Yes, I know, practicalities for an entrepreneur are about as exciting as Sunday morning in Rhyl in the pouring rain, when the only thing open is the public loo, but it must be said. There is free help available out there, seek it out and get help with things that could come back to bite further down the line. Things such as Accounts, Tax, NI Contributions, Legal Structure, I could go on.

Expert Advice

Get a mentor (or mentors)
A word about mentors. No matter how talented and committed you are, there is someone out there who has already been through the pitfalls you haven't even imagined yet. Someone who has been there and experienced the pain and delight of self-employment, who has been through the tears and the laughter probably more than once and that someone will be more than happy to help you. They won't be there to drive your business, but they will help you steer it and you in a focussed direction.

When you find a mentor make sure it is someone who has your best interest at heart who will tell you as it is, whether that is good or bad and has the same passion and commitment in their job as you do in yours; but please don't choose anyone who is doing it for a job. In other words, choose someone for whom helping you is 'who they' are, not 'what they do'. One more thing, make it a symbiotic relationship, in other words, do something for them too.

Building a network of people (Team) with the same values and passion for the business and complimentary skills to yours can open doors that you can only dream of banging your head against by working alone. As the saying goes, 'No man is an island' (except maybe the Isle of Man). A word of warning about partnerships here though, if your gut says all is not well, trust it, it's true.

CV – Background

At the outset of your business it is difficult to show a background to gain support. It is therefore imperative that you show that you and your partners if you have them are credible and have the experience and knowhow to deliver on your business plan. Don't set it out like a normal CV that you send to an employer. List your background and skills which relate to the business you are creating. Put yourself in the shoes of the backer and make this document a compelling reason for them to believe in you and give you their support.

Chamber of Commerce

The local Chamber of Commerce is a great source of information and advice and if you are able it may be worth joining. They can help with policies, HR, Legal issues and of course networking. Remember that to get the most from the Chamber of Commerce you need to be an active member. Not always easy when you are on your own but remember the title!

Local Authority

Believe it or not my friend, your local council isn't just there to collect your community tax, issue parking fines and miss your bin collections. Oh no, your local authority is usually keen to attract business into the area so that they can collect your corporation tax, issue business fines and charge you for your business bin collections.

Gov.uk

This is a major source of information for all sorts of things from business support to taxing your car. Have a play on this site and type in some questions.

Sector specific Businesses

It's always worth speaking to people who have done it before you. Choose someone who is operating away from your area. Not many people will help you set up a rival business if you are moving in next door. People are usually willing to show you around their business and help you if you approach them politely and you will likely form alliances, which will help you develop ideas for your business along with more tangible help. You may even be able to work together in some way. These guys know the pitfalls that you could fall into and they may be helpful in pinpointing something that you haven't even thought of.

Google

You don't know how lucky you are starting out these days. OK I realise I'm going to sound ancient now but back in the day, not so long ago if we wanted to know something, we had to ask our friends, visit the library, and even there we couldn't ask specifics, we had to research. In 1979 a movie came out called Close Encounters of the third kind. It was about contact with aliens. In one scene, scientists are trying to decipher a coded message from space. One guy realises the message is a set of map co-ordinates. They run into an office and collect a giant globe, they carried the globe into the lab to look for the coordinates where they think the aliens will land. No asking Google in those days.

Everyone carries a smartphone with them now. For the young entrepreneurs out there just starting out, you are so lucky, you are the first generation who have the world's knowledge literally at your fingertips. What do people use this vast resource for most? Selfies, I despair. If you have a smartphone just about anything you need to know is there for the asking. Whether you want to know how far the moon is from the earth, or who invented dynamite, or where was Einstein born or calculating the best route to *anywhere*. It's the same for business, how to format management accounts, who and where are your competitors or potential customers, how to price your service etc. You don't have to even type it in anymore, or even get out of bed. Just ask Siri, Cortana, Google and an answer will appear. Exciting times so don't be afraid that you lack knowledge.

We can look anywhere in the world but what's the first thing we look at on Google Earth? Our own house.

Sales

Sales are not just for people or companies that make things or buy and sell goods or services. You also sell yourself, in fact as an entrepreneur 'selling yourself' is what you do most. People buy into 'you' first, then your, idea, project, company etc. If they believe in you, people are always willing to back you whether they are funders, bank managers, investors or customers.

By the way, you must never think of selling as how much you can get. Selling should be a mutually beneficial arrangement. You offer a product or service with as much benefit to the customer/client as possible and the customer pays you a fair price, they are happy with. This way you should always gain residual income and repeat business, everyone is happy.

There are thousands of books on sales techniques out there so I'm not going to dwell on this subject, but I think the best advice I can offer here is 'be true to yourself and your customers'. Satisfied customers tend to keep quiet after the transaction, but unhappy customers shout it from the rooftops. Be warned.

Website

How do you attract a partner? You do your hair, make up, a nice dress/suit and put a smile on your face. Your website is the window to the world and it's the first thing a funder (or business people you want to work with) or customers will look at to see if you are an attractive proposition to work with. Get the best site you can, it's not so much about the money, its about the design so look at the web designers previous work.

If you don't have the skills to develop a website find someone who will help. There are sites now where you can build a decent off the shelf site but think long and hard about the pages you need, the content and the image you want to portray long before you begin to build the site. Put it on paper first. This goes for your Facebook account and other social media such as linked-in.

Last words of encouragement

Throughout this book there has been one main theme running through it, sometimes overtly, sometimes subliminally. The fact that 'you can do this'. There's only one real prerequisite and that is that you must be willing to go all in 'until' you get there. There are so many examples and encouraging words I hope with all my heart that at least one of the stories resonates with you and makes a small 5-degree shift to start you on your entrepreneur journey or whatever journey you choose. That small shift today will be the catalyst for a giant change further down the line.

Remember the secret all entrepreneurs know? (It's never about can or can't, it's always about will or won't. A mindset not a skillset). The leap of faith you need to take to get you started in your venture, not faith in God necessarily but in yourself. Incidentally, if you do believe in God, you must believe that he wants the best for you and will protect you the way you would protect your children. Here we explored Will Smiths words, Indiana Jones' and Adam Peaty's story to name a few.

We looked at Social Conditioning using the example of the baby elephants (Break the chains) and Pavlov's dog experiments. How we are 'conditioned' to conform to what others think we should be, have or do. What do you want to be, have or do? That's important too. We looked at how people put us down and use psychological leverage to stop us growing. Sometimes openly through jealousy, sometimes unconsciously through love.

I shared the note I wrote to my younger self, why don't you try it and write a note to your younger self. I used the medium of poetry, but you can use your style. It doesn't even have to be a letter, maybe a picture, cartoon or a song even? We discussed

96

not worrying too much about competition or certificates and the importance of turning a Wishision into a decision it is important to move forward with intent until you succeed, and you will.

We explored Adversity (mine and many, more famous and successful entrepreneurs). Remember the fire that burned down my business. Thankfully adversity doesn't usually come in extreme forms like this too often, but small cumulative things over time can really get us down. We have all experienced it and mark my words, we all have it coming again so we also looked how to develop a Bullet proof mindset when the shit hits the fan. The positive thing we can take from this is the strength it gives us once we have overcome adversity. We looked at a positive spin on what we consider to be negative emotions. We can't avoid them, but we can decide what they mean to us and therefore how to deal with them.

One last thing my friends. If you are serious about taking this giant leap don't let anyone put you off. You know in your heart if you are ready, determined, skilled and passionate enough to do this, whatever 'this' is for you. If the answer is yes, then go for it. If you fall on your ass then it won't be failure, it will be learning, and it won't be due to not trying, will it? Everybody has challenges, catastrophes even, use these events to fuel your passion and drive you to greatness.

You are truly a miracle. There has been estimated to be between 100 – 200 billion galaxies, with the sun the right place in the universe in the right place in our solar system, to support life on earth, the perfect distance from the Sun. You live on a planet with over 7 billion people, an estimated 107 billion people have ever lived, consisting of 150 thousand generations and your ancestors have made it through being hunted by Sabre tooth Tigers and other animals, wars, famines, extreme weather, pandemics and modern-day dangers until your parents met.

If just one of your ancestors died before having children or meeting a partner, then 'you' wouldn't exist. 1 in 200 million chance alone that your parents met, then from 1 trillion sperm cells from your father, one of which found that one egg from your mother. The conservative estimated probability of you being born is around **400 trillion to one.**

After all this, you have a brain with 100 billion neurons which are capable of incredible ideas and feats. You are truly unique.

When Elvis Presley called Sun records to ask to make a record for his mother's birthday, the receptionist asked him "who are you like"? He said I'm like nobody". She asked, "who do you sound like"? He said I don't sound like nobody mam. You, my friend, are like nobody else, you are *you* with all your experiences, problems, joy, pain, knowledge and ideas. People who try to tell you that you are not special or unique really don't realise how incredible you really are. Even sadder, they don't realise how incredible they are if only they knew.

Heroes don't have super powers and super strength. They don't fly around wearing their underwear on the outside, saving the world. Heroes are men and women like you, mothers and fathers, people who go through trials and bad times, people who get scared, upset, afraid and devastated but they don't live there. Heroes try again and again without having any guarantee of success because it's the right thing to do.

True heroes pick themselves up time after time to carry on when all they want to do is give in. Real heroes carry on despite how bad they feel, and they inspire their friends, family, children and ultimately, complete strangers through actions and deed. Real heroes are just like you my friend, don't ever think otherwise.

It is an incredibly powerful moment when you finally realise that you have changed beyond your recognition of who you used to be. When something happened that would have previously knocked you down, and this time you just handled it, took it in your stride, even got a buzz from the situation.

From that day on my friend you will never return to old limitations. Nobody knows apart from you if the prize is worth the pain. If you will use what drives you, to move anywhere except back. I hope to meet you one day (maybe at one of our events) and hear about your incredible journey. Here's wishing you the greatest of luck.

You've got this.